# ROYAL MUSEUMS GREENWICH
# Handbook

# Ahoy! Hello! Welcome!

## THE ROYAL MUSEUMS GREENWICH HANDBOOK

is the perfect companion guide for explorers of Greenwich like you.

Take this book with you as you walk around Greenwich Park or the National Maritime Museum. Let it be your guide as you step into the Queen's House, explore the Royal Observatory and climb aboard *Cutty Sark*.

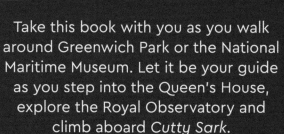

Put your skills to the test and navigate the seas on page 29.

Mary Prince introduces her story on page 20.

Have you read all there is to read about the National Maritime Museum? Take the quiz on page 30.

Think you know your nautical words? Try the maritime word search on page 28.

Want to test your knowledge on all things Queen's House? Turn to **page 38** for a quiz!

Henrietta Maria welcomes you to her home on **page 34.**

Ruth Belville explains why she was known as the 'Greenwich Time Lady' on **page 46.**

The Royal Observatory needs your help! Can you work out the names of the Astronomers Royal on **page 50** and relabel the objects on **page 51**?

Can you imagine what it would be like to live and sail on the *Cutty Sark*? Write a postcard to your friends or family on **page 62.**

Captain Woodget describes his life on board Cutty Sark on *page 58.*

Are you now a seasoned sailor? Do you think you know the ropes? Take the *Cutty Sark* quiz on **page 63** and find out.

# WELCOME TO GREENWICH!

Royal Museums Greenwich is home to four fascinating places. They are all part of Maritime Greenwich, which is a UNESCO World Heritage Site. That means it is a unique and important place!

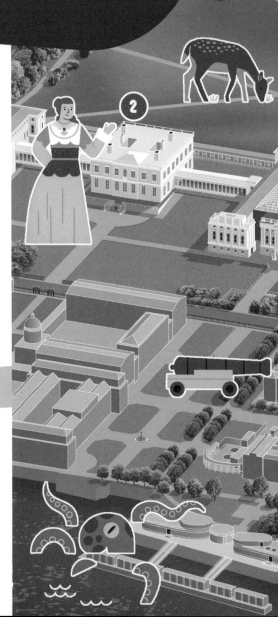

### National Maritime Museum

Start your seafaring adventure at the Great Map. Which exciting gallery will be your first port of call? Delve into tales of exploration and endeavour and discover how different cultures are connected to the sea.

### The Queen's House

There's plenty to uncover at this royal villa. Find out about its intriguing history and admire its art and architecture – and perhaps you'll catch a glimpse of the ghost that's said to haunt the famous Tulip Stairs!

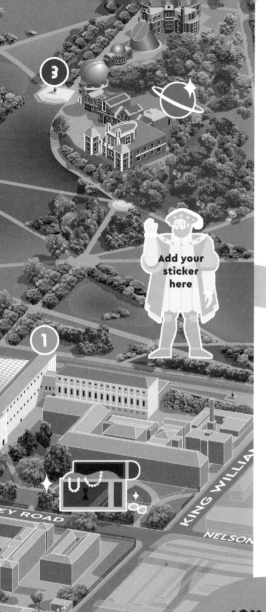

### Royal Observatory Greenwich

Climb up the hill to this world-famous observatory and discover why Greenwich is known as the 'home of time'. Learn about the astronomers who lived and worked here and become a space explorer at a planetarium show.

### *Cutty Sark*

The world's last surviving 'tea clipper' has endured enormous waves, dangerous icebergs and even a fire. Walk its historic decks, and learn about its crew, cargo and adventures.

## WHAT'S IN A NAME?

There has been a settlement at Greenwich since Anglo-Saxon times. Its name was Green Wic, which means 'green village'. Today, the 'w' has become silent, so we say 'GREN-itch'.

# GREENWICH THROUGH TIME

From the mid-1400s, Greenwich was home to a royal palace – a place where kings and queens loved to spend time relaxing. Since then, the site has gone through many extraordinary changes.

## 1491

One of England's most famous monarchs, King Henry VIII, is born at Greenwich Palace. He builds a banqueting hall for grand feasts and holds huge jousting tournaments in the grounds. Henry marries two of his six wives at Greenwich, and his daughter, the future Elizabeth I, is born here in 1533.

## 1613

The wife of James I, Anne of Denmark, orders the Queen's House to be built. It is completed in 1635 for Queen Henrietta Maria.

## 1660

Greenwich Palace is in bad condition following the English Civil War. Charles II demolishes it to make way for a new palace, which is never completed. In 1675, he orders the Royal Observatory to be built 'for perfecting the art of navigation'.

In 1937, the National Maritime Museum opens, including the Queen's House. In 1954, *Cutty Sark* is moved to the dry dock at Greenwich as a visitor attraction, and the Royal Observatory is opened to the public in 1960.

**1954**

The Greenwich Hospital buildings become a college for the training of Royal Navy officers. The college stays there until 1998.

**1874**

The site of Greenwich Palace is turned into a hospital for wounded sailors. The magnificent building is designed by architect Christopher Wren.

**1694**

## There's so much to see and do.

Can you find all of the things below? Tick off or add a sticker when you've found them!

Nelson's coat

Cutty Sark's figurehead, Nannie

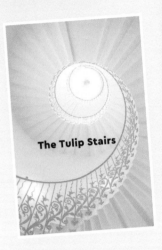

The Tulip Stairs

A telescope

The Shepherd Gate Clock

A flag

A cannon

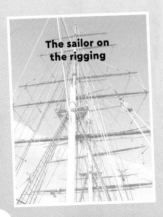

The sailor on the rigging

The Prime Meridian line

Cutty Shark at the Cove playground

# NATIONAL MARITIME MUSEUM

# INCREDIBLE OCEAN

The ocean teems with amazing plants and creatures – but did you know it supports human life too? From the air we breathe to the water we drink, we could not exist without it!

## WATER ON EARTH

The ocean is a vast body of saltwater that covers more than two-thirds of the planet. It is divided into five ocean basins.

As the Sun heats the ocean, water vapour rises into the sky to form clouds. Eventually, the water falls to Earth as rain or snow – helping plants to grow and giving us water to drink. Some of this water flows into lakes and rivers, to be carried back to the sea.

We need oxygen to survive. But did you know that more than half our oxygen comes from the ocean and marine plants such as seaweed?

## CLIMATE CONTROL

The ocean is constantly moving. Beneath the surface, powerful currents transport warm water to cold regions, and cold water to tropical regions. This helps to regulate the climate around the world.

## EXPLORING THE DEPTHS

Deep beneath the waves are great trenches, extraordinary aquatic forests and huge mountains. Incredibly, only about a quarter of the sea floor has been mapped – and there are still many mysteries to be solved!

New technology is leading the way. Robot submersibles can reach areas too dangerous for human divers, while sonar systems can map the ocean floor.

Seascape paintings by John Everett

## OCEAN UNDER THREAT

Today, the ocean faces many challenges. Climate change is causing sea temperatures to rise, while pollution is harming plants and animals. We rely on the ocean – and the ocean needs us! It is up to everyone to look after this incredible environment.

At the bottom of the Pacific Ocean lies the 2,543-km- (1,580-mile-)long Mariana Trench. Its deepest part, The Challenger Deep, is nearly 11 km (7 miles) below the ocean surface – which is deeper than Mount Everest is tall!

# VOYAGES IN THE PACIFIC

Did you know that the Pacific is a vast sea of islands, an ocean that covers a third of Earth's surface and full of vibrant cultures? Tangata Moana, meaning 'the people of the ocean' in Māori, have lived in the region for over a thousand years, creating rich traditions of voyaging and diverse ways of living.

Add your sticker here

Pacific Ocean

## EUROPEAN ADVENTURERS

In 1520, Portuguese navigator **Ferdinand Magellan** (1480–1521) became the first European to reach the Pacific. In the eighteenth century, explorers such as **Captain James Cook** (1728–79) charted numerous islands and coastlines.

**Tupaia** (about 1725–70) was an Ariki (chief) and a brilliant navigator from Ra'iatea, Tahiti. He joined Captain Cook's first expedition on board the ship *Endeavour*. Cook depended on Tupaia's incredible knowledge of winds, currents and star paths, and his ability to communicate with the Māori people of New Zealand.

This is **Adi Yeta**, she is a *drua* (canoe) built in 2014–15 using traditional Fijian boat-building techniques that have been in use for a very long time.

**Captain Cook** made three voyages to explore the Pacific. Sailing great distances, he mapped the coast of New Zealand and east Australia, crossed the Antarctic Circle and became the first European to set foot on Hawaii. When a fight broke out between his crew and the Hawaiians, he was killed, alongside four of his men and as many as 30 Hawaiian people.

*A painting of Hawaii in 1779*

We need to be careful with the words we use. The Kānaka Maoli, the Indigenous people of Hawaii, have lived on the land for over a thousand years. When Europeans first arrived they encountered a well-established society, they did not 'discover' the land.

# TOOLS OF THE TRADE

One of the biggest challenges for early European explorers was not getting lost! Navigators relied on their knowledge of the Sun and stars and used simple instruments to note their position. Today, modern technology has transformed life at sea.

Add your sticker here

## MAPS AND CHARTS

Imagine how difficult it was for early explorers and mapmakers to work out the shape and structure of landscapes and coastlines. The National Maritime Museum has more than 30,000 maps and charts in its collection. It's fascinating to compare early maps to those of today.

*World map from 1573*

## COMPASS DIAL

This beautiful dial was made in 1569. It could be used as a compass, sundial, Moon phase calendar and to find the times of high and low tides. It was made by England's first instrument maker, Humfrey Cole.

## SEXTANT

This instrument, dating from 1791, was used to measure the angle between the Sun (or the Moon) and the horizon. The readings it gave helped sailors to work out a ship's latitude – its position north or south of the Equator.

*This sextant is made of polished brass with a wooden handle.*

## SIP-AND-PUFF HELMET

Natasha Lambert was the first person to sail across the Atlantic using this incredible technology. She was born with quadriplegic cerebral palsy, a condition that affects her limbs and speech. This helmet allows her to control the boat's steering and adjust the sails with her breath and tongue.

# POLAR PIONEERS

The regions near the North and South Poles are called the Arctic and the Antarctic. Explorers to these icy places have faced treacherous landscapes, bitter cold and long hours of winter darkness.

## LOST EXPEDITION

In 1845, British explorer John Franklin (1786–1847) set sail with two ships, *Erebus* and *Terror*, for the Canadian Arctic. His mission was to map a North-West Passage from Europe to Asia and undertake scientific research. However, the ships vanished without trace, and all 129 men were lost.

Add your sticker here

The Inuit – one of many different communities of Indigenous people living in Alaska, Canada and Greenland – have inhabited the Arctic for thousands of years. Their knowledge and skills helped researchers to locate *Erebus* and *Terror* – the two shipwrecks were finally discovered in 2014 and 2016.

*This is a killuutuniq – a type of Inuit knife. This one was made from material left behind by the Franklin Expedition, perhaps from one of the boats or wooden boxes. The bone in the handle is from Inuit hunting of animals.*

# TRAPPED IN ICE

In 1914, Ernest Shackleton (1874–1922) set sail on *Endurance* with 27 men. The plan was to cross the Antarctic, but the ship became stuck in ice and sank. Eventually, the crew managed to reach a remote island in three lifeboats. Shackleton and five others then set out on an 1,287-km (800-mile) sea voyage to the nearest inhabited island. Thanks to his incredible leadership, all the men were rescued.

Today, the polar regions are being affected by climate change. In the Arctic, scientists are working closely with Inuit peoples to understand the effects of global warming. Teams of scientists work in the Antarctic all year round to study how increasing temperatures are affecting the sea ice.

# RICHES AND POWER

As Europeans explored the world, they began to claim land, or 'colonies', for their countries. Nations built powerful empires – but the people who had their land, goods and resources taken from them often suffered.

Add your sticker here

## FRANCIS DRAKE

Tudor explorer Francis Drake (about 1540–96) was a 'privateer', which meant he had royal permission to attack enemy ships. He sailed right around the world, visited large parts of the Americas and claimed land for England. Celebrated by the English as a swashbuckling hero, Drake was feared by the Spanish as a ruthless pirate, while the Indigenous people saw him as a threat to their land.

# EAST INDIA COMPANY

In 1600, Elizabeth I allowed a group of merchants to form the East India Company. For 250 years, this business earned great riches by trading with India, China, Indonesia and the region now known as Iran. Its ships brought goods such as spices, cotton, silk and tea back to Britain.

The East India Company became a hugely powerful organisation, with armed ships and forces. Eventually, it controlled large parts of India. By the time the company ended, in 1858, the British government directly ruled India.

*Draw your own pirate flag*

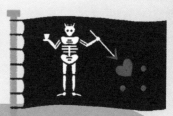

Ruthless pirates prowled the seas, attacking merchant ships and stealing their precious cargoes. In the late 1600s and early 1700s, many pirate captains – such as William Kidd and Blackbeard – became hugely successful and wealthy.

# ENSLAVEMENT AND RESISTANCE

Between 1500 and 1800, millions of people from Africa were kidnapped and enslaved, transported across the Atlantic and forced to work in Europe's colonies. This is known as the Transatlantic Trade in Enslaved Africans.

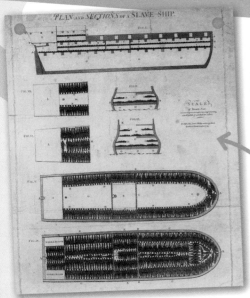

The conditions on the ships were terrible and many people died during the voyage. Those who survived were sold to wealthy landowners and put to work.

*This drawing shows how people were crammed on board the ship Brooks. By law, a ship of this size was pemitted to carry 454 people but Brooks sometimes carried as many as 740 enslaved people.*

A huge amount of money was made from the Transatlantic Trade in Enslaved Africans. This wealth is still visible throughout Europe today.

My name is Mary Prince, and I would like to tell you about slavery and how the Transatlantic Trade in Enslaved Africans finally came to an end. You see, I was once enslaved – but like many people I fought for my freedom.

I was born in Bermuda in 1788, the child of enslaved people. From the age of 12, I was sold several times. I worked as a housemaid and laboured under a hot sun. My feet were covered in painful boils and I was often whipped. Eventually, my owners went to Britain, taking me with them.

Although slavery was no longer allowed in Britain, my owners refused to set me free. So, I asked the Anti-Slavery Society for help and was given shelter. An author agreed to write down my story and it became a book: *The History of Mary Prince, a West Indian Slave.*

## ROAD TO FREEDOM

Many enslaved people and communities resisted enslavement, while others managed to escape. Anti-slavery activists, called 'abolitionists', made speeches and wrote pamphlets. Mary Prince was the first Black woman in Britain to speak out against enslavement, and her story helped people to see that it was cruel and unjust.

ABOLITION OF COLONIAL
# SLAVERY

Abolitionists created objects, like this glass seal, to call for the end of the Translantic Trade in Enslaved Africans. Britain abolished slavery in 1807 but those already enslaved were not freed until much later.

# THE ROYAL NAVY

In the 1500s, Henry VIII began to build dockyards and a fleet of powerful warships. This was the start of Britain's organised fighting force at sea, the Royal Navy.

## RULING THE WAVES

For much of the 1700s and early 1800s, Britain and France were at war with each other. The Royal Navy's largest warships had room for around 800 men and more than 100 cannons. They carried everything the crew needed for months at sea.

**Admiral Lord Horatio Nelson** (1758–1805) rose to fame during the French Revolutionary Wars (1792–1802). In 1805, he led an attack on a fleet of French and Spanish ships at the Battle of Trafalgar. It was a famous victory for Nelson, though he was killed by a musket ball during the fighting.

*Have you seen the ship in a bottle by the artist Yinka Shonibare outside the National Maritime Museum?*

## LIFE AT SEA

Life for naval seamen could be tough. Despite the benefits of regular pay, meals and friendship, their floating home was damp and crowded. They faced injury and death in battle, and punishments like flogging with the 'cat-o'-nine tails'.

## UNIFORM

The Royal Navy first introduced uniforms in 1748 – more than 200 years after the Navy first formed! Naval uniform has had a big influence on fashion and popular culture ever since. In 1799, an article in *The Times* mentioned the colour 'Navy blue' for the first time.

*This is one of the first naval uniform patterns from 1748. Only officers had formal uniforms at the time.*

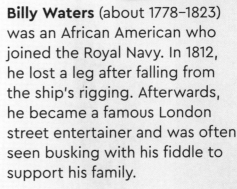

**Billy Waters** (about 1778–1823) was an African American who joined the Royal Navy. In 1812, he lost a leg after falling from the ship's rigging. Afterwards, he became a famous London street entertainer and was often seen busking with his fiddle to support his family.

# WAR AT SEA

Draw your own 'dazzle' patte

The Royal Navy played a crucial role in both the First and Second World Wars. Its warships took part in key battles and protected important sea routes and merchant ships carrying vital supplies.

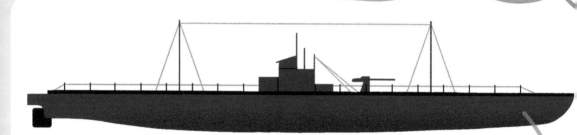

## CONVOYS

'U-boats' were among Germany's most feared weapons during the First World War (1914–18) and the Second World War (1939–45). These submarines prowled the oceans, attacking and sinking thousands of merchant ships. 'Convoys' – groups of merchant ships sailing together under the protection of warships – became an important part of the Royal Navy's tactics.

## THE BATTLE OF JUTLAND

This ferocious battle, fought off the coast of Denmark in 1916, was the largest sea battle of the First World War. Around 151 British warships fought against 99 German ships. At the end of the fighting, both sides claimed victory.

From 1917, Britain used dazzle-painted ships to confuse the enemy. Merchant ships were painted with stripes and swirling patterns, making it difficult for enemy vessels to estimate their size, speed and position.

## THE WRENS

The Women's Royal Naval Service (WRNS) was formed in 1917. At first, the 'Wrens' did jobs such as cooking or secretarial work. During the Second World War, they took on roles that had previously been thought of as men's work. Their responsibilities included driving, operating radar equipment, providing weather forecasts and codebreaking. The WRNS became part of the Royal Navy in 1993.

*This drawing is one of 14 illustrations by a Wren called Gladys E. Reed.*

# STORIES AND LEGENDS

What do you think of when you imagine the ocean? It can be calm, beautiful and awe-inspiring – but it can also be a place of mystery and danger. It's not surprising that the sea is connected to many stories and superstitions from across the ages.

Add your sticker here

## MONSTERS OF THE DEEP

In the medieval period, maps often featured drawings of sea monsters, both real and imagined. Sailors sometimes returned from their travels with accounts of terrifying sea monsters. Perhaps these sightings were of real-life giants, such as squid or whales?

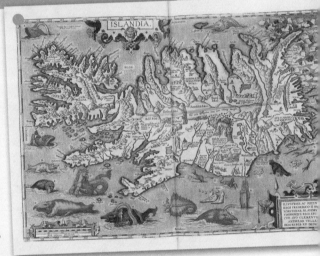

## PROTECTION AT SEA

Have you ever wondered why old ships had a carved figurehead at the front? You can see a collection of these striking sculptures beneath the hull of *Cutty Sark* and in the Museum. Sailors took great care of a ship's figurehead, believing it protected the vessel from violent storms and other perils.

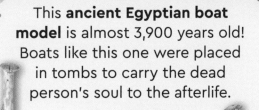

The hundreds of objects in the Museum's 'Sea Things' gallery all have a tale to tell. Do you have a favourite?

This **ancient Egyptian boat model** is almost 3,900 years old! Boats like this one were placed in tombs to carry the dead person's soul to the afterlife.

A young sailor climbs the rigging on this **sperm-whale tooth**. On long journeys, whalers passed the time by engraving art – called 'scrimshaw' – on whale bones and teeth.

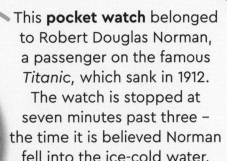

This **pocket watch** belonged to Robert Douglas Norman, a passenger on the famous *Titanic*, which sank in 1912. The watch is stopped at seven minutes past three – the time it is believed Norman fell into the ice-cold water.

More than 5,000 items have been recovered from the wreckage of the *Titanic*.

```
I P J J E Y C H Z G C F C U G
G Z M S G F V H F E O E I B T
Q V L K A W B A A R L C T E E
A Z C Z Y D S K N R I M C E E
K V R Y O O F A K F T X R C B
C C W J V H W Z I C N S A Z X
K O H W T L D C I L D F Y B B
D M Z J F N A T J Z O D D E A
S P W G P P C T J A H R Y H V
Y A H A C R R X I K B W S K B
M S L T A A C K O F E X B L A
I S H T D R A Y K C O D E X N
K U N E X P E D I T I O N C H
I A F H T W J G U D Q Z I S Z
Q C H O I S G M A P S W X E E
```

Add your
sticker here

## CAN YOU FIND THESE HIDDEN WORDS?

ANTARCTIC    DOCKYARD    PACIFIC

ARCTIC    EXPEDITION    SAILORS

CHARTS    MAPS    TRADE

COMPASS    NAVY    VOYAGE

# CAN YOU NAVIGATE YOUR OWN VOYAGE?

START

YOU MADE IT!

1. What fraction of the world's surface does the Pacific Ocean cover?

   a) a quarter

   b) two thirds

   c) one third

2. What is the name of the tool early seafaring navigators used to measure the angle between the Sun (or the Moon) and the horizon to work out their position at sea?

   a) compass

   b) sextant

   c) telescope

3. What was the name of the explorer who set sail on the ship *Endurance* for an Antarctic mission in 1914?

   a) Ernest Shackleton

   b) Captain James Cook

   c) Sir Francis Drake

4. What was the name of the British company formed by merchants in 1600 that traded across the world?

   a) Maritime Trading Company

   b) Gentleman Adventures Company

   c) East India Company

5. What is the name of the carved sculpture often found at the front of old ships?

   a) sculpturehead

   b) figurehead

   c) frontispiece

I scored...                    /5

# THE QUEEN'S HOUSE

# FIT FOR A QUEEN

The Queen's House is a place where art, architecture and history all come together. This 400-year-old building has served as a royal home, an art studio and a school for orphaned children.

## 1613

James I (1566–1625) gives Greenwich Palace to his queen, Anne of Denmark. The royal gift is meant as an apology for shouting at her after she accidentally shoots his favourite hunting dog! In 1616, Anne asks architect Inigo Jones to build her a magnificent house – but sadly she dies before it is completed.

## 1635

The Queen's House – now belonging to Henrietta Maria, the wife of Charles I – is finally completed. The queen fills its rooms with wonderful art. In 1644, the Civil War forces her to flee to France and, in 1649, Charles I is executed.

Charles II offers artists Willem van de Velde the Elder and Younger a studio in the Queen's House. The famous father-and-son duo produce celebrated sea paintings.

**1673**

Willem van de Velde the Elder

**1640**

For more than 100 years, the Queen's House serves as the Greenwich Park Ranger's official home.

**1807**

The house becomes an orphanage school for the children of naval seamen. By 1843, there is a large training ship in front of the house to prepare boys for a life at sea.

## THE QUEEN'S HOUSE TODAY

In 1937, the Queen's House was opened to the public as part of the National Maritime Museum. Inside, you can discover exciting works from both old masters and modern artists, as well as fascinating echoes of the house's past. What will you find?

# HOUSE OF DELIGHT

My name is Henrietta Maria and I was the first queen to use this special house. Once you've admired its fine exterior and wandered through its grand rooms, you will understand how it came to be known as a 'House of Delight'!

Inigo Jones (1573–1652), the house's architect, was inspired by Italian classical architecture. In fact, this house was the first building in England to be constructed in the 'Palladian' style.

At the front of the house, elegant 'horseshoe' steps lead up to a terrace. On the other side, a covered balcony looks over Greenwich Park. The columns give the house the feel of a classical Roman temple.

Anne of Denmark used the side of the house facing the park as the front but I used the horseshoe terrace as my entrance. Which would you choose?

At the centre of the house is the Great Hall. It was built to form a perfect cube! Can you see how the marble floor mirrors the shapes on the ceiling above? Nine colourful paintings once adorned the ceiling but they were removed by 1708. In 2016, an eye-catching gold-leaf design by artist Richard Wright was painted in their place.

Create your own ceiling design.

The spiralling Tulip Stairs are not only a marvel of architecture but also a wonderful work of art. Despite the name of the stairs, the flowers on the iron rail are in fact lilies – the royal flower of my home country, France.

35

The Queen's House contains more than 450 works of art. There are portraits of famous royals, an extraordinary model of a warship and a thought-provoking painting of migrants at sea.

**Ship of Fools, 2017, by Kehinde Wiley**
Four young migrants are adrift on a stormy sea in this oil painting. Their boat has a tree instead of a mast. For centuries, people have crossed seas in search of a better life. This painting reminds us of the dangerous journeys made by migrants today and throughout history.

*Olaudah Equiano*, 2006, b
**Christy Symingto**
This famous African activi
wrote a book about h
experiences as an enslave
person. On the back of the bu
is a diagram of a crowded sla
ship – a reminder of the terrib
suffering that enslaved Africa
people endure

Equiano worked (
ships that carrie
him across the wor
and into battle durir
the Seven Years W
Later, he was ab
to purchase his ov
freedom. He travelle
to Britain as a fr
man and settled
London where
became a leadir
figure in t
abolition movemer

**St Michael, 1669**
For many years, experts weren't sure what ship this model represented – then an eagle-eyed scholar spotted its similarity to drawings of a Royal Navy warship called the *St Michael*. This makes it the world's earliest model of a known ship!

Can you see how the Queen's hand rests on a globe? Both Elizabeth and the artist wanted to show her power and command of the seas.

**The Armada Portrait**, about 1588, by an unknown artist
This magnificent portrait of Elizabeth I celebrates England's defeat of the Spanish Armada – an invasion fleet sent by Philip II of Spain. The small scene on the left shows English ships before victory, while the gloomy scene on the right shows wrecked Spanish ships.

1. King James I gave Greenwich Palace to which queen as an apology?

a) Elizabeth II

b) Henrietta Maria

c) Anne of Denmark

2. Which father-and-son painting duo had a studio in the Queen's House?

a) Willem van de Velde the Elder and Younger

b) Orazio and Lomi Gentileschi

c) Marcus Gheeraerts the Elder and Younger

3. What was the name of the architect who designed the Queen's House?

a) Arlo Jones

b) Inigo Jones

c) Christopher Wren

4. What is the name of the famous staircase found in the Queen's House?

a) Bluebell Stairs

b) Rose Stairs

c) Tulip Stairs

5. What nickname was the Queen's House given when Henrietta Maria lived there in the 1600s?

a) House of Delight

b) House of Wonders

c) House of Magnificence

I scored...   /5

# ROYAL OBSERVATORY

Add your
sticker here

# SPACE AND PLACE

Today, ships rely on satellite navigation to find their way – but things weren't always that easy! In the age of exploration, navigation errors led to many shipwrecks and lost lives. In 1675, Charles II ordered that the Royal Observatory be set up to improve navigation at sea.

**Add your sticker here**

## FLAMSTEED HOUSE

This building, built in 1676, is the oldest part of the Royal Observatory. It was named after John Flamsteed, the first Astronomer Royal to live and work here. For 40 years, he measured and recorded the position of many stars.

To work out your exact position on Earth, you need two measurements. Latitude is your north-south position, and longitude is your east-west position. In the 1600s, sailors calculated latitude by measuring the height of the Sun and stars, but there was no reliable way to measure longitude. This was the puzzle that the Royal Observatory's astronomers set out to solve.

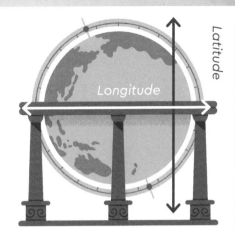

## MARGARET FLAMSTEED

Many women have played an important role at the Royal Observatory, though their contribution hasn't always been recognised. John Flamsteed's wife, Margaret, studied maths and astronomy and worked as his assistant. After his death, she helped to publish his work.

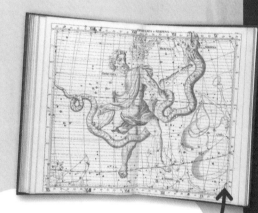

John Flamsteed's Atlas Coelestis, *which Margaret helped to publish.*

Next to Flamsteed House, you can find a camera obscura. Can you see how it captures images of the traffic moving along busy Romney Road? John Flamsteed used an early camera obscura to safely observe an eclipse of the Sun.

# THE LONGITUDE CHALLENGE

In 1714, the British government offered a huge reward to anyone who could find an accurate way to measure longitude at sea. The prize was worth millions in today's money – a sign of how important the issue had become!

## TIME AND PLACE

There is a close link between longitude and time. Because Earth rotates 360 degrees in 24 hours, a change of 15 degrees longitude results in a time difference of one hour. Sailors knew they could work out longitude by comparing local time with the time back home – but because pendulum clocks were unreliable at sea, keeping track of time was very difficult.

## 1735

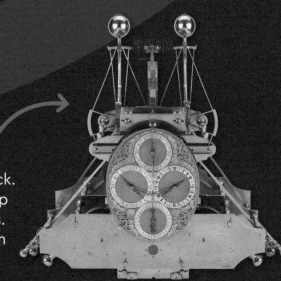

Clockmaker John Harrison (1693–1776) develops the first sea clock. The 'H1' has special balances to keep it running smoothly on choppy seas. For more than 20 years, he works on improving his design.

# 1759

Harrison completes his fourth timepiece, the 'H4'. It looks like a large pocket watch and is very accurate in tests – but expensive to make. However, it's a game-changer that eventually wins Harrison the longitude prize!

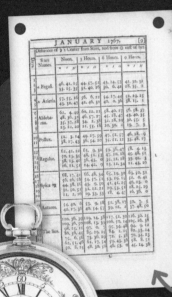

# 1767

The fifth Astronomer Royal, Nevil Maskelyne, measures the Moon to predict its position months ahead. His book, the *Nautical Almanac*, proves very useful at sea, though navigators must still do complicated sums to work out longitude. This method is known as the 'lunar distance method'.

# 1771

To prove that the success of Harrison's H4 wasn't a fluke, Larcum Kendall (1721–90) makes a copy called the 'K1'. Captain Cook takes it on his second voyage to the Pacific in 1772.

# 1780

Better designs by John Arnold and Thomas Earnshaw result in the first modern chronometer, an accurate timekeeper that was used for 150 years.

# FAMOUS FACES

Between 1676 and 1948, ten Astronomers Royal lived and worked at the Royal Observatory. Over the years, many other astronomers and skilled assistants supported their work.

**George Biddell Airy (1801–92)**
The seventh Astronomer Royal lived at Flamsteed House with his wife, Richarda, and their many children. He designed a powerful telescope called the Airy Transit Circle – it was used to make 600,000 observations of the night sky.

**Edmond Halley (1656–1742)**
Perhaps you have heard of the famous Halley's Comet? In 1705, Edmond Halley – who became the second Astronomer Royal – correctly predicted the comet would return to Earth's skies in 1758. The comet will next be visible on 28 July 2061!

Astronomers align their telescopes with an imaginary line running from the North to the South Pole, called a 'meridian'. This helps them to track objects in the night sky. In 1884, the **Greenwich Meridian** – as defined by the Airy Transit Circle telescope – was chosen as the reference point for measuring longitude around the world. It is zero degrees longitude, the starting point for measuring east and west.

**Annie Maunder (1868–1947)**
This maths whizz worked as a 'lady computer' for the eighth Astronomer Royal, William Christie – and went on to become an expert in solar eclipses and sunspots. As a woman, Maunder faced many obstacles in her working life, but is now remembered as a trailblazing astronomer.

I discovered...

........................................

........................................

........................................

........................................

Imagine you are the Astronomer Royal. Draw your face in the frame and describe your discovery!

# GREENWICH TIME

You may have heard of 'Greenwich Mean Time', or 'GMT' – but what does it mean? My name is Ruth Belville, and I once ran a famous 'time service' in London. I'm going to explain why Greenwich is known as the 'home of time'.

## GMT

Up until the mid-1800s, towns across Britain kept their own local time by observing the Sun. But as the railways grew, a single, uniform time was needed so that trains could run smooth schedules. The time at Greenwich – Greenwich Mean Time (GMT) – became the standard.

Add your sticker here

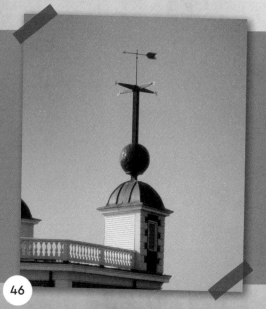

## TIME BALL

One of the earliest public time signals was the Greenwich Time Ball. It was placed on top of Flamsteed House in 1833, where it could easily be seen from the river. Every day, the ball dropped at precisely 1 p.m., so that ship navigators could set their chronometers to the correct time.

# SHEPHERD GATE CLOCK

Have you seen this famous clock outside the gates of the Royal Observatory? The original clock, installed in 1852, was the first clock to show GMT directly to members of the public. It was controlled by electrical signals from a clock inside the Observatory, called the Shepherd Motor Clock.

The Shepherd Gate Clock can be hard to read because it uses Roman numerals and has 24 hours on its face rather than the usual 12. Do you know what time this is?

From 1892, I was known as the 'Greenwich Time Lady'. Once a week, I visited the Royal Observatory to check my pocket watch against the Shepherd Gate Clock. Then I travelled to around 50 clockmakers across London to sell them the correct time! This service came to an end in 1940.

THE TIME

SHEPHERD PATENTEE
53 LF LONDON
GALVANO-MAGNETIC

# MAPPING THE STARS

The Royal Observatory was set up to improve navigation at sea, but it's also been important for exploring the Universe. Today, you can admire groundbreaking telescopes or journey through the night sky in an exciting planetarium show.

Add your sticker here

## GREAT EQUATORIAL TELESCOPE

This historic telescope, installed at the Observatory in 1893, was used to research 'double stars' – a pair of stars that orbit each other. Step beneath the instrument's 'onion dome' roof and marvel at its extraordinary size!

## STAR SIBLINGS

Astronomer William Herschel found fame when he discovered the planet Uranus in 1781. Within the gardens of the Royal Observatory, you can see the remains of the 12-metre (40-foot) reflecting telescope he built at his home. William's sister, Caroline, was also a pioneering astronomer – she did important work on John Flamsteed's star catalogue and was the first woman to discover a comet.

# CAPTURING STARLIGHT

In the mid-1800s, astronomers at Greenwich began using new technology to photograph the sky. Gradually, 'astrophotography' became an important part of the Observatory's work. In 2007, a competition was set up to find the Astronomy Photographer of the Year. Each year, the spectacular winning photographs are displayed at the National Maritime Museum.

*M63: Star Streams and the Sunflower Galaxy,* by Oleg Bryzgalov

Explore the mysteries of space at the **Peter Harrison Planetarium**. Astronomers and leading scientists can take you on a journey through the Solar System, fly you to distant galaxies or show you the birth of a star. Each day, there are different shows, sessions and talks to give you an out-of-this-world experience!

Fill in the missing letters to complete the names of the former Astronomers Royal at the Royal Observatory.

1.  J_HN F__MST_ED
2.  _DM_ND H_L_EY
3.  JA__S B__DLEY
4.  NAT_A_I_L _LI_S_
5.  _EV_L M_SK_LYN_
6.  JO__ P__D
7.  GE___E BI_DE_ AI_Y
8.  WIL___M H__RY MA__NEY C__IST_E
9.  _RA_K WAT_ON D_SON
10. HA_O__ SP_NC_R _ON_S

# CAN YOU HELP LABEL OUR COLLECTION ITEMS?

1. Portrait of Margaret Maskelyne

2. Mariner's compass

3. The *Nautical Almanac*

4. John Harrison's H4

5. The Time Ball

6. Nocturnal

7. Astrolabe

8. John Harrison's H1

1. Which king founded the Royal Observatory to improve navigation at sea?
   - a) Henry VIII
   - b) James I
   - c) Charles II

2. Which two measurements do you need to work out your exact position on Earth?
   - a) tropical and subtropical
   - b) equatorial and polar
   - c) longitude and latitude

3. What was the name of the clockmaker who eventually won the longitude prize?
   - a) Thomas Earnshaw
   - b) John Harrison
   - c) Edmond Halley

4. What is the name of the imaginary line used by astronomers to align their telscopes and which runs from the North to the South Pole?
   - a) meridian
   - b) equator
   - c) latitude

5. At what time does the Greenwich Time Ball drop every day, originally so that ship navigators could set the correct time?
   - a) midnight
   - b) midday
   - c) 1 p.m.

I scored... /5

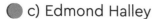

# CUTTY SARK

# BUILT FOR SPEED

The famous *Cutty Sark* is the world's last surviving tea clipper. The ship was built in 1869 in Dumbarton, Scotland, to carry tea from China to Britain as quickly as possible – for that it needed speed as well as space.

*The sharp bow was designed to slice through the water.*

*The 32 sails, supported by three tall masts, caught plenty of wind power!*

*A 'clipper' means a fast vessel, or one that can 'go at a clip'. Cutty Sark was certainly that, reaching speeds of more than 17 knots (31 km/h [19 mph]).*

*The long, narrow hull, made of wood and iron, was covered in a brass alloy. This prevented damage to the ship from sea creatures such as barnacles.*

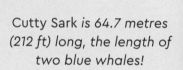

*Cutty Sark is 64.7 metres (212 ft) long, the length of two blue whales!*

## JOCK WILLIS

*Cutty Sark* was built for John 'Jock' Willis, a Scotsman who had taken over his father's shipping business. It was his ambition that *Cutty Sark* would be the fastest tea clipper of all!

*The name 'cutty sark' comes from a famous poem by Robert Burns called 'Tam O'Shanter'. It features Nannie the witch who is wearing a 'cutty sark', a term for a short undergarment or shift.*

*Cutty Sark* was designed to beat rival ships at sea, but it also needed enough room for its crew and precious cargo.

Photo taken by Captain Woodget

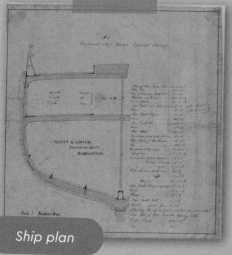

Ship plan

Skilled dock workers packed the tea tightly into the **Lower Hold**. The least valuable tea was placed at the bottom and sides in case it was damaged by water.

The middle or **'Tween Deck** was also used for cargo and storage.

'Tween Deck

The crew lived and worked on the **Main Deck**. This is where they slept, ate, climbed the rigging and steered the ship.

Main Deck

# TEA AND WOOL

Tea was first brought to Britain from China in the 1650s. As its popularity spread, it went from being a luxury item to the nation's favourite drink. Tea was big business – and clipper ships played an important role in the tea trade.

## TEA RACES

The Victorians didn't just want tea – they wanted it to be as fresh as possible! Clipper ships loaded the latest tea from China into their holds. Then the vessels competed against each other to be the first to dock in London.

*People used to keep tea in a caddy like this one.*

In 1872, *Cutty Sark* and *Thermopylae* raced from China to Britain. *Cutty Sark* led the race, until its rudder was lost in a storm off the coast of South Africa. *Thermopylae* reached London after 115 days at sea, and *Cutty Sark* arrived seven days later.

*Can you count how many sails Thermopylae has? Do you think it has more or less than Cutty Sark?*

On a typical journey, *Cutty Sark* carried goods such as wine, brandy and marmalade to ports in China. On the way back, the ship carried around 600,000 kg (1,322,773 lb) of tea – enough to make more than 150 million cups!

## END OF THE TEA CLIPPERS

In 1869, the Suez Canal was opened. This passage, linking the Mediterranean with the Red Sea, cut thousands of miles off the journey from China to London. However, sailing ships were unable to use the canal – and steamships soon took over the tea trade.

Add your sticker here

## WOOL VOYAGES

In 1883, *Cutty Sark* began transporting wool from Australia. The clipper became famous for its sailing times between Australia and Britain – no other ship could match its speed!

# ALL ABOARD!

My name is Captain Woodget and it's a pleasure to welcome you on board *Cutty Sark*. I captained this ship on ten voyages between Britain and Australia. Under my command, it became the fastest in the wool trade!

*This is a photo of three of the crewmembers serving under Captain Woodget in 1887. From left to right: James Weston, Third Mate; G. Thompson, Steward; James Robson, Cook.*

*James Robson was the longest-serving cook, and petty officer on Cutty Sark, sailing on ten voyages. Born in China, he was apparently found as a baby and adopted by a sea captain and his wife.*

## MEET THE CREW

The crew of around 26 men worked in four-hour shifts called 'watches'. It was all hands on deck – the men climbed the rigging in all weathers, cleaned out the animal pens and mended the sails. The youngest crewmember, an apprentice called John William Edwin Mayall, was just 14.

Most of the men slept in bunks in shared deckhouses, while the two mates and I had cabins at the back of the ship. There was little time for leisure – though sometimes I rode a bike or rollerskated on the 'Tween Deck for exercise!

Pigs on board a ship called Magdalene Vinnen

The cook prepared our meals in the small galley. The food on board had to last months at sea, so we ate a lot of salted beef, dried peas and ship's biscuit. Pigs and chickens were kept on the Main Deck, which gave us occasional fresh meat and eggs.

## DANGER!

To catch the best winds, *Cutty Sark* sailed as far south as possible. That meant facing ferocious gales and huge icebergs. Once, a massive wave broke over the ship and smashed the doors of the deckhouses! But it was worth the risk – Captain Woodget's first voyage from Australia to Britain took a record-breaking 73 days!

# CUTTY SARK TODAY

By 1895, *Cutty Sark*'s wool-trading days had come to an end – but it was not the end of the clipper's adventures! After sailing under the Portuguese flag for more than 25 years, the ship finally came to Greenwich.

## FERREIRA

After being sold to a Portugeuese firm, *Cutty Sark* was renamed *Ferreira* – and continued to carry cargo around the world. In 1922, a retired sea captain and his wife, Wilfred and Catharine Dowman, bought *Ferreira*. They brought the ship to Falmouth in Cornwall for its restoration and also set up a school to train new sailors.

More than 350,000 people visit Cutty Sark each year.

## FIRE ON BOARD

*Cutty Sark* was opened to the public in 1957. In 2007, a fire broke out on deck. Luckily, the ship had been closed for repairs so many of the ship planks and most of its fixtures and fittings had been removed. Less than 5% of the original fabric of the ship was damaged. It was yet another chapter in *Cutty Sark*'s dramatic story!

As you explore *Cutty Sark*, there are plenty of fascinating things to look out for...

Add your sticker here

Near the centre of the 'Tween Deck, look up to see *Cutty Sark*'s **registration number** stamped into the iron frame.

The ship's figurehead is the witch, **Nannie**, from Robert Burns' poem 'Tam o' Shanter'. What do you think she is wearing?

You can see the **ship's bell** on the Main Deck. Eight strikes let the crew know when it was time to start or end a period of duty, or 'watch'. The bell was also used as an alarm call – on a stormy night, it was all hands on deck!

# SEND A POSTCARD

Imagine you are a crewmember on board *Cutty Sark*. Write a postcard to friends or family describing your new life at sea! What might you have seen? What is your day-to-day life like on a tea clipper?

*Don't forget to draw a postage stamp!*

POSTCARD

# QUIZ

1. In what year did *Cutty Sark* first set sail?
   - a) 1840
   - b) 1850
   - c) 1870

2. What product did *Cutty Sark* start transporting from Australia in 1883?
   - a) cotton
   - b) tobacco
   - c) wool

3. How old was the youngest known crewmember on *Cutty Sark*?
   - a) 9
   - b) 12
   - c) 14

4. What year did *Cutty Sark* open to the public as a museum site?
   - a) 1954
   - b) 1957
   - c) 1968

5. What is the name of *Cutty Sark*'s figurehead?
   - a) Nannie
   - b) Mummy
   - c) Frankie

I scored...

/5

# ANSWERS

## Page 28 Word search:

## Page 29 Maze:

## Page 30 National Maritime Museum quiz answers:

c. one third
b. sextant
a. Ernest Shackleton
c. East India Company
b. figurehead

## Page 38 Queen's House quiz answers:

c. Anne of Denmark
a. Willem van de Velde, the Elder and Younger
b. Inigo Jones
c. Tulip Stairs
a. House of Delight

## Page 50 Royal Observatory Greenwich activity answers:

JOHN FLAMSTEED
EDMOND HALLEY
JAMES BRADLEY
NATHANIEL BLISS
NEVIL MASKELYNE
JOHN POND
GEORGE BIDDEL AIRY
WILLIAM HENRY MAHONEY CHRISTIE
FRANK WATSON DYSON
HAROLD SPENCER JONES

## Page 50 Royal Observatory Greenwich label answers:

In order of appearance (left to right)

3, 4, 5, 8, 1, 2, 7, 6,

## Page 52 Royal Observatory Greenwich quiz answers:

c. Charles II
c. longitude and latitude
b. John Harrison
a. meridian
c. 1 p.m.

## Page 63 *Cutty Sark* quiz answers:

c. 1870
c. wool
c. 14
b. 1957
a. Nannie